Linux Mastery

The Ultimate Linux Operating System and Command Line Mastery Guide

INTRODUCTION

I want to thank you and congratulate you for downloading the book, "Linux Mastery - The Ultimate Linux Operating System and Command Line Mastery Guide"

While not as popular as Windows—at least, for some—Linux is definitely one of the most reliable Operating Systems around—and the best part about it is that it's free, so you don't really have to pay for anything just to get it, and you also wouldn't have to go for counterfeit types of Operating Systems just because you could not pay for the legal copy. More than anything, Linux can be used for a variety of applications. Whether you're opting to create a better system for business, or just want to be more creative and play around with things, Linux can help you do a great job.

This book contains proven steps and strategies on how to make use of Linux, whether for work or play, understand the commands that you have to use, choose distributions, and understand exactly why Linux matters—and more.

Surely, after reading this book, you'll be adept about Linux—and you will have an easy time using it for your needs.

Read this book now, and find out how!

Thanks again for downloading this book, I hope you enjoy it!

CONTENTS

CHAPTER 1 WHAT IS LINUX?

So, what is Linux, actually?

For starters, Linux is a free and open-source Operating System, based on UNIX and PSOIX codes. In short, it is free to download, and free to use, and was originally based on the paradigm of Intel x86. In fact, out of all Operating Systems, Linux has the largest base that has been installed, compared to the rest. This is why a computer or device that works on Linux works fast, and are sometimes even compared to those amazing supercomputers! This is because Linux gets to be tailored to any kind of system where it's being used for—compared to other operating systems that work best on a certain kind of device alone. This so happens because of the so-called open source software collaboration that can support various kinds of libraries and directories.

http://cdn1.mos.techradar.futurecdn.net//art/software/Linux/Best%20di
stro/linux-distros-im-650-80.jpg

Early Beginnings

Back in 1969, the UNIX Operating System—also known as the forefather of Linux—was created at the AT & T Bell Laboratories, with C-Programming basics, and high availability of languages that could be used for porting purposes. With that kind of background, this OS became the most relied-on operating system of business and school administrators.

However, certain controversies happened when an anti-trust case prevented UNIX from continually being used for businesses, but since its developers—and its supporters—believed that there's still more to UNIX than what people think, they decided to develop the GNU Kernel—and it was because of this that LINUX finally came to fruition.

Enter Linux

With the help of its principal author, Linus Trovalds, and his principle of finding a truly functional Operating System that everyone can use, he decided to work on the GNU Kernel. He wanted something that people, whether they're professionals or just wanting to use the computer and other devices for entertainment, could really use. He then began to upload files created from the Kernel to the FTP Server, and wanted to call it "Freax", but his collaborators and other professionals at the time didn't think it was a good idea, and so playing with his name, Linux was born in 1991!

1. To create an Open-Source Programming Language, so it would be free, and everyone would be able to contribute to its development;
2. To create something that's as good as its predecessors and competitors, but make sure that it is easy to understand, and that it is intuitive;
3. To create a programming language that would be useful for everyday tasks, and;
4. To simply create a programming language that could be compared to plain English, when readability is concerned.

When it was first published (to be used) in 1991 as Version 0.9.0, core datatypes, functions, and inheritance such as str, dict, and list were already available. In 1994, Version 1.0 was released and it involved reduce, filter, map, and lambda, amongst others, and in 1995, Van Rossum continued to work on developing Linux while at the Corporation for National Research Initiatives in Virginia!

In 2000, the BeOpen Linux Labs team was established, and Version 1.6 of the language was put out, with important bug-fixes. Another version called Version 2.0 was released in 2008, followed by 3.0—which could coexist with the other!

Linux Now

Today, Linux is partly responsible for helping the world work like it should. From people who only work with computers at home, to larger feats such as NASA using Linux-powered computers, it is no surprise why Linux is

The Ultimate Linux Operating System and Command Line Mastery Guide

getting the attention of many—and today, you have the chance to learn about it, and more!

CHAPTER 2 WHY LINUX?—THE BENEFITS OF LINUX

Apart from what was mentioned earlier, why is it that you have to choose Linux? What exactly can you get from it?

Well, there are loads of advantages that you can get if you choose to use Linux as your Operating System, some of which are as follows:

Amazing Security

One of the best things that people love about Linux is that compared to other operating systems, it is quite secure. You wouldn't have to buy those costly anti-virus systems because on its own, Linux could do all the virus and security checks that you need, and in fact, you will learn a lot about this in the last chapter of this book.

What you have to understand is that since Linux is an open source system, even if some programmers can create bugs or anything that might be "harmful" to your computer, you can expect that a counter-attack is just within reach. In fact, if you can research or study about it, you might even create one yourself.

Great Hardware, and Software, too

If you're one of those people who still use those big, clunky, old computers, or if you computer doesn't have much memory or processing power, you'd be glad to know that Linux could work for it, too. In fact—and in relation to what was mentioned above—even if your computer does not have firewall or any of those "safety precautions", you can still expect it to work without fail—mainly because Linux was really created to "work", and not to give you so many ridiculous problems.

Now, when it comes to software, Linux also has a lot to offer. While Windows offers one version for each app—for example, Text Editor, Microsoft Word, Windows Movie Maker, Linux has hundreds and thousands of options that you can choose from—and that you can get for free. So, say, you're going to search for a text editor, you can just search for that, and guess what? A lot of options will be presented to you, so you can choose the one you're most comfortable with, and the one you think would yield the best results. This also means that Linux Software has greater

The Ultimate Linux Operating System and Command Line Mastery Guide

usability and readability, therefore, it won't be alienating to anyone the way software from other operating systems are—especially if you have to pay a lot for them!

You Have the "Power of Choice"

As aforementioned, you have the choice to decide on what kind of software you like to use. You also have the choice to design your desktop or device the way you want, simply by using Linux. It makes the act of using the computer or any device you have more personalized—more like something you'd feel comfortable with, and one that would be quite manageable for you.

The problem with other Operating Systems is that somehow, they feel so hard to maneuver—and that's not good, especially if you're a beginner in the whole process. Now, not only will you be able to learn what needs to be done easily, you also won't have a hard time when it comes to using your computer the way you want—and the way you want it to look like.

Flexibility

Flexibility is also one of the best things about Linux. With Linux, you won't have to deal with hoop-jumping, piracies, scams, or anything that would make it hard for you to "take control" of any given situation. It also has forums that you can join to think about security and other issues, if those are bothering you, or are making you confused.

Multiple Program Paradigms

Linux also supports various program paradigms, such as:

Object-Oriented Programming. This makes use of the concept of objects, such as fields, data, and data structures and their attributes.

Imperative Programming. Meanwhile, Imperative Programming involves the use of statements to modify the state of a program. Simply put, it deals with how the program achieves its result, as opposed to what the program should achieve.

Functional Programming. And, finally, Linux also deals with functional programming, or the paradigm that deals with mathematical computations and functions to develop an outcome.

It's Compatible for Most Devices!

You do not have to buy a new device just to use Linux. Again, and as mentioned earlier, it might even work for old computers—which is amazing because some people have issues when it comes to letting their old computers and devices go—and that's something you would not feel for this one. Its kernels work for old and new devices, so there's no need to upgrade anything or buy something new.

It's Easy to Use and Understand

Sometimes, t's so hard to find a product or a service that really, ultimately works well for you. But, when it comes to Linux, that happens almost instantly—and that's amazing especially if you're new to the whole open-source paradigm!

And, It Gives You Lots of Choices!

Linux is all about helping you make the most out of what's installed in your computer. It is not alienating. If you don't like something, it gives you the chance to look for something else—find something better. And with that in mind, it becomes easier for you to do what you should—and make use of it in the manner that you know is best for you.

CHAPTER 3 CHOOSING A DISTRIBUTION

The next thing you have to do is choose your own Linux Distribution. Basically, these are just the different versions of Linux that you can choose from, and yes, all of them are the same, when it comes to being Operating Systems, but they differ when it comes to aesthetics, and the way they "work".

Basically, there are various distributions to choose from, but there are seven that are the most trusted, and these are:

Ubuntu

http://cdn3.mos.techradar.futurecdn.net//art/software/Linux/Best%20di stro/ubuntu-650-80.jpg

Ubuntu is possibly one of the most popular distributions of Linux, and is deemed to be the best to choose if you're new to Linux, or have not tried it before. Ubuntu has amazing easy-to-install repositories, and is quite customizable—perfect for art and media practitioners, or those who are just extremely careful about what they see onscreen. The problem with Ubuntu is that compared to other distributions, it does not work as great with mobile devices—which can be a bit of a problem, especially if you're the type who's on your mobile device all the time.

Souls

http://cdn3.mos.techradar.futurecdn.net//art/software/Linux/Best%20di
stro/solus-1-650-80.jpg

Souls has that modern feel, and is in fact, somewhat new as it was released only in 2012—a time when Ubuntu was mostly used in schools and businesses. Some say that the best thing about Souls is its aesthetic feel, because it really has that elegant, nice-to-look-at feel to it. One thing, though, is that there aren't too many "Soul Communities" around yet, so if you get to have problems with this distribution, you might have to look for the solution yourself.

Mint Cinnamon

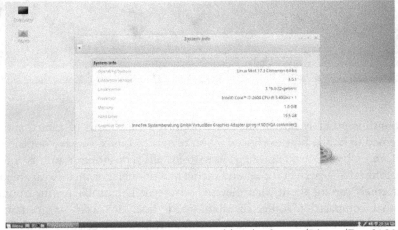

http://cdn4.mos.techradar.futurecdn.net//art/software/Linux/Best%20di
stro/linux-cinnamon-650-80.jpg

Such a fresh-sounding name, isn't it? Well, Mint Cinnamon actually has that fresh and light feel as it mostly makes use of white and gray for aesthetics. It's quite the minimalist distribution of Linux—perfect for people who do not like seeing a lot of pizzazz and anything too colorful on their screens. The best thing is that its repositories are the same as Ubuntu's, so you won't have much of a hard time trying to understand them, and its UI is also less-demanding—so it wouldn't be too taxing on your computer, and on you who's going to be using it. Mint Cinnamon is also deemed to be great for beginners, because as aforementioned, there's not much to understand about it—and you really don't have to give yourself a hard time for it, too.

Ubuntu Studio

http://cdn3.mos.techradar.futurecdn.net//art/software/Linux/Best%20di
stro/ubuntu-studio-650-80.jpg

As the name suggests, this incarnation of Linux is perfect for producers, musicians, sound engineers, designers, and artists who need to work with various kinds of multimedia, and who need computers or devices that are tailored for that purpose—Ubuntu Studio definitely makes that easy. Having been around since 2007, this one has a multi-track, digital recorder and sequencer named "Ardour" that's being relied on by many artists around the globe. The best thing about the said recorder is that it synthesizes guitar and other instruments that have been used, making sure that your final output would be really pleasing to the ears, and not at all hard to deal with. Therefore, you'd get to create projects that are of professional quality—without spending much for it.

Arch Linux

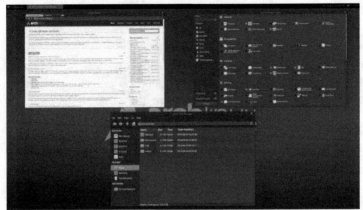

This one is deemed to be perfect for professionals because it is something that you have to work with and customize on your own. In fact, it does not even come with as many applications as other distributions do, which means that you do have to know what you're doing. With this, you have to apply the "Keep it Short and Simple" philosophy, because downloading too much might just make you confused. Find what you really want, and then prune or get rid of those you feel won't matter to you, so that your screen won't be too cramped, and so you can make the most out of this distribution. However, what's good about it is that you may learn a lot, so even if you may have a bit of a hard time in the beginning, rest assured, you'd get past that, and experience what Arch Linux really is about!

Chrome OS

The Ultimate Linux Operating System and Command Line Mastery Guide

http://cdn4.mos.techradar.futurecdn.net//art/TRBC/Software/ChromeO S/chromedesktopapps-hero-650-80.jpg

It's said that this is one of the main and closest renditions of the early Linux GNU Kernel, but that it has actually exceeded expectations, and is proving to be one of the most reliable Linux distributions. It has since then been repurposed into a working environment on its own, mostly because it's used to make certain Google Apps, and works fast even if you use applications that take up much space, such as Photoshop. It will make your work much more manageable, but the issue is that there are certain applications that are not available on this distribution that you can find in other Linux distributions. It's also the kind of distribution that works better offline, so that could be hassle if you're always connected to the web, but you can make certain updates or upgrades with minimal fees, anyway.

Elementary OS

http://cdn2.mos.techradar.futurecdn.net//art/software/Linux/Linux-luna-elementary-os-4-650-80.jpg

And finally, there's the Elementary Distribution. Not only is it one of the most aesthetically-pleasing versions of Linux, it's also highly functional, and some say has that resemblance to the Mac—perfect for multimedia artists and those who work with high-end applications, as well. In fact, it may as well be your perfect Windows or Mac replacement, in the event that you are looking for something new that you can rely on quite well. It also has an amazing line of pre-installed apps, and even a custom web-browser that can really personalize the way you use Linux.

CHAPTER 4 PREPARING TO INSTALL LINUX

Before installing Linux, make sure that you are mindful of what it poses for you first. Basically, these are:

Linux isn't just Linux.

If you've been reading the earlier chapter properly, you would understand that Linux isn't just "one" operating system, or one version that continually evolves over time, the way Windows does. Linux is something that contains different versions within it, and that works with GNU.

If you're confused as to what GNU is, you can think of it as a collection of applications, schedulers, text editors, compliers, and anything else that you can work with in a command line. When you think of Linux now, you can think about it as a "kernel"—and a kernel may contain multitudes within it. This matters when it comes to hardware, because while Linux offers an amazing collection of software, it doesn't have much hardware. So, in the event that you find something wrong with hardware, you have to find the solution on your own, or find the answer from a list of Linux's collected answers—and with over 200 variations of Linux, you'll surely be able to find what you need sooner or later. The lack of hardware would also make you more discerning of your choices. It will help you question whether what you've got in front of you is really good, and if it's something that you actually need—you won't just download everything and ruin your computer.

You would have a fun time customizing and accessorizing your desktop.

Gone are the days when you'd just install an OS, and that's that. You just have to wait for the latest update, or try something new if you don't like how it looks like onscreen. However, with the help of Linux, you get to customize your desktop, and turn it the way you want it to be. This happens because Linux works with what's called a "Desktop Environment". This means that you can let your browser, and other programs be displayed on your desktop all at once so you won't have to close your Word Processor while trying to compute something, watching your favorite show, and the like. It really puts "multi-tasking" to a test—and helps you access a modernized version of using the computer exactly for what you need it for.

The Ultimate Linux Operating System and Command Line Mastery Guide

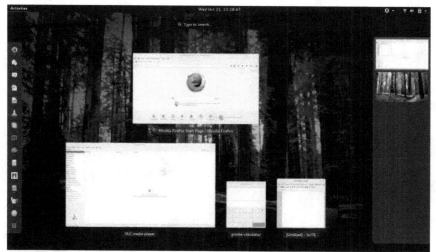

http://cdn.mos.cms.futurecdn.net/56d8a1d50e1d0c1cfc9262fd5243d40b-650-80.png

Aside from that, there's also a Gnome3 Activities panel which allows you to choose from various Linux Desktop Environments. You might even choose more than one, if you just want to have fun with your desktop and not make it monotonous. You can then configure this the way you want.

There are different devices, files, and folders.

Linux is not Windows—it is far from that. Of course, seeing a different bunch of files and folders onscreen might be confusing at first, but do remember that even if the names or the looks are different, they work in the same paradigm—albeit in a much improved manner.

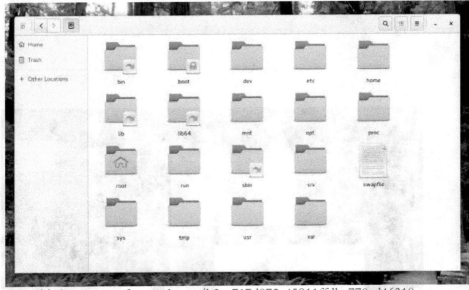

Basically, the file system starts with the root, also known as a "simple path"—or where everything stems from, and where they go. So, in case you're traveling and you get to bring your laptop with you, you can choose one port for files on the go, and another for files at home—and this would not disintegrate your system. This is good because it is less confusing, and it allows you to focus.

Apart from the root and the ports, things look a bit the same as you're used to, but you might also notice that they're cleaner now, or that they are easier on the eyes. These file extensions are meant to help you as a user, which means that while they may be confusing on the get-go, you won't have a hard time trying to learn about them—and you'd appreciate them sooner or later.

There are great software repositories.

You know how with Windows, you often have to search the web for the applications or programs that you need? And, chances are, if you're not using Google Play or the App Store, you'd have to filter what you've found because they might not be legit, or might not be working? Well, you wouldn't experience that with Linux.

The Ultimate Linux Operating System and Command Line Mastery Guide

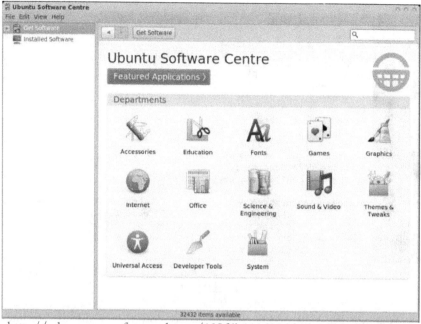

http://cdn.mos.cms.futurecdn.net/139f6b1116326daebac6bba8c925660f-650-80.png

Linux has some of the best software repositories—packages that you can choose from to determine what would work best for you, depending on your preferences. From the Software Center, you can choose from various kinds of packages, and rest assured that all of these are working. Getting viruses from this is not common, and if it happens, you can easily find the antidote, too—and that's definitely perfect, especially if you're only starting out with Linux!

It'll help you appreciate and understand the "open-source" paradigm.

Free software doesn't have to be something that's not of high quality, or that so easily malfunctions. With the help of Linux, you'll realize that sometimes, the best things in life really do come free. It'll help you get a different perspective on things, especially when technology is concerned, and you'll see your computer and other devices as more than just virtual machines, but stuff that you can personalize and can really help you out in various ways.

And, it's safe for your device!

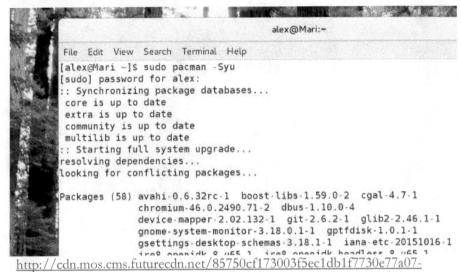

Linux is not the kind of OS that works so slow that it already becomes detrimental for the health of your computer, or any device you have. This also happens because of the fact that you can easily search for, and use antidotes for bugs, viruses, and other software damage from Linux itself. It won't leave you alone in the dark, and won't make you feel lost, especially if you are still a beginner, or have not used this operating system before. So, instead of seeing your device die, and looking for hard to understand, and expensive ways of solving the problem, you can do it yourself now. It works fast, and as reiterated in this book, is easy to understand—so no more terminal illnesses for your devices from this point on.

The Ultimate Linux Operating System and Command Line Mastery Guide

CHAPTER 5 INSTALLING LINUX

Of course, before using any distribution of Linux, it is essential that you install it first. To make that happen, here's what you have to do:

Download the latest version from the official website. (https://www.linux.org/).

There, you will find an MSI Package—just double click the file and follow the installation procedure that you will see onscreen. Take note that even if you already have another version of Linux on your system, you can still download a new one as it installs in a new path, with the number of Linux versions that you have. (i.e., C:\Linux\27) This would not get in conflict with the other versions you have.

Add directories to PATH for it to easily be found. (i.e., C:\Linux\27 to PATH, etc)

You can also try the following script in Powershell (just look for this label):

C:\Linux27/ ; C; Linux27\ Scripts

[Environment]:: SetEnvironmentVariable ("Path", "$env:Path;C:\Linux27\Script")

```
vivek@nas01:~$ su -
Password:

 * keychain 2.7.1 ~ http://www.funtoo.org
 * Found existing ssh-agent: 2160
 * Found existing gpg-agent: 2186
 * Known ssh key: /root/.ssh/id_rsa

root@nas01:~# apt-get install screenfetch
Reading package lists... Done
Building dependency tree
Reading state information... Done
The following NEW packages will be installed:
  screenfetch
0 upgraded, 1 newly installed, 0 to remove and 0 not upgraded.
Need to get 0 B/41.4 kB of archives.
After this operation, 196 kB of additional disk space will be used.
Selecting previously unselected package screenfetch.
(Reading database ... 72532 files and directories currently installed.)
Preparing to unpack .../screenfetch_3.6.5-1_all.deb ...
Unpacking screenfetch (3.6.5-1) ...
Processing triggers for man-db (2.7.0.2-5) ...
Setting up screenfetch (3.6.5-1) ...
root@nas01:~# logout
vivek@nas01:~$
```

http://s0.cyberciti.org/uploads/cms/2015/09/ubuntu-debian-linux-apt-get-install-screenfetch.jpg

Version 2.0 (if the above does not work)

You can also try opening the Command Prompt (Start> All Programs> Accessories> Command Prompt)

Then, on the command prompt window, type:

set path=%path%;C:\Linux27\ and press Enter, and install package Simplejson. (You can download it from this link: http://pypi.linux.org/pypi/simplejson)

Extract package into download directory. After doing that, you should see something like this on your screen:
C:\Users\pdxNat\Downloads\simplejson-2.1.6\

```
[    8.920947] input: HDA Intel PCH Headphone as /devices/pci0000:00/0000:00:1b.0
/sound/card0/input11
[    8.921089] mei 0000:00:16.0: PCI INT A -> GSI 16 (level, low) -> IRQ 16
[    8.921096] mei 0000:00:16.0: setting latency timer to 64
[    9.249847] Synaptics Touchpad, model: 1, fw: 7.5, id: 0x1e0b1, caps: 0xd00073
/0x240000/0xa0400
[    9.283798] input: SynPS/2 Synaptics TouchPad as /devices/platform/i8042/serio
1/input/input12
[    9.422009] scsi 6:0:0:0: Direct-Access     Multiple Card  Reader      1.00 PQ:
 0 ANSI: 0
[    9.423558] sd 6:0:0:0: [sdb] Attached SCSI removable disk
[    9.767983] Adding 2097148k swap on /dev/sda3.  Priority:-1 extents:1 across:2
097148k
[   10.540393] XFS (sda4): Mounting Filesystem
[   10.773454] XFS (sda4): Ending clean mount
[   21.358256] alx 0000:02:00.0: irq 44 for MSI/MSI-X
[   21.358260] alx 0000:02:00.0: irq 45 for MSI/MSI-X
[   21.358263] alx 0000:02:00.0: irq 46 for MSI/MSI-X
[   21.359557] alx 0000:02:00.0: enp2s0: NIC Link Up: 100 Mbps Full
[   21.363343] ADDRCONF(NETDEV_UP): enp2s0: link is not ready
[   21.363933] ADDRCONF(NETDEV_CHANGE): enp2s0: link becomes ready
[   29.219796] fuse init (API version 7.16)
[   31.707722] enp2s0: no IPv6 routers present
```

http://s0.cyberciti.org/uploads/cms/2015/09/ubuntu-debian-linux-apt-get-install-screenfetch.jpg

Once you see that, open a new command prompt and type:
cd downloads\simplejson-2.1.6 or

c:\Users\pdxNat\Downloads\simplejson-2.1.6 to get a result of:

c:\Users\pdxNat\Downloads\simplejson-2.1.6>

The Ultimate Linux Operating System and Command Line Mastery Guide

Open another command prompt and type linux setup.py install

Open IDLE (Start > Linux 2.7 > IDLE (Linux GUI)> and then type Insert Simplejson

That's it! You're all set!

CHAPTER 6 USING LINUX FOR WORK AND PLAY

As mentioned earlier, Linux can be used for a variety of applications—and can work for both work, and play.

For Work

On the serious side, Linux can work for supercomputers. In fact, it is the OS used for all supercomputers after the demise of Earth Simulator, a supercomputer of the past. NASA also uses Linux for all their computers and applications—so it's really something that helps bring earth closer to space, and helps a lot of people learn more about the universe! In some offices, Linux is used to help create an efficient system of inputs and outputs—minus the slowness that other Operating Systems bring.

Linux also works for embedded systems, or any device that uses "real-time" mechanisms. For example, if you're going to watch "TV" but have no television and can only use devices such as BusyBox, you can expect that what's being fed on real television screens would also be captured by the BusyBox—in real time! This means you wouldn't have to miss out on anything—so if you're a media practitioner, this can definitely aid you in your work.

Linux is also used for some mobile devices to help make sure that virtualization becomes easy and prevalent, and helping the user get the best virtual experience possible—perfect for advertisers who make use of augmented reality in their ads. Apart from that, Linux is also used in most servers, especially dynamic sites that work under LYCE and LYME, and those that use LAMP, respectively. It also works for cloud computing, as well as for managing services and infrastructures, and the like.

For Play

And of course, Linux works great for fun purposes, too! It can work as a human interactive device, and place to play your favorite games on Android and other mobile devices, because Linux can work as an amazing gaming platform, with gaming greats such as Valve choosing Linux as a platform for its applications starting in 2012. The famous Steam also uses Linux, and helps customers understand that it's actually not alienating—and it can help one play games faster, and in a more enjoyable manner.

In short, Linux is around for mostly anything that you need—and that's why it wouldn't hurt for you to try it.

The Ultimate Linux Operating System and Command Line Mastery Guide

CHAPTER 7 GETTING TO KNOW COMMANDS

There are various commands that can make the way you use Linux even easier and better. You can learn more about them below.

Main Keywords/Commands:

zip
Package and compress files.

yes
Print a string until interrupted

xz
Compress or decompress .xz and .lzma files

xdg-open
Open URL or file in user's preferred application

xargs
Execute utility, pass constructed argument list/s

write
Send a message to another user

whoami
Print the current user id and name (`id -un`)

who
Print all usernames currently logged in

while
Execute commands

which
Search the user's $path for a program file

whereis
Search the user's $path, man pages and source files for a program

wget

Retrieve web pages or files via HTTP, HTTPS or FTP

wc
Print byte, word, and line counts

watch
Execute/display a program periodically

wait
Wait for a process to complete •

vmstat
Report virtual memory statistics

vi
Text Editor

vdir
Verbosely list directory contents (`ls -l -b')

Verbosely
list directory contents (`ls -l -b')

uuencode
Encode a binary file

uudecode
Decode a file created by uuencode

users
List users currently logged in

usermod
Modify user account

userdel
Delete a user account

useradd
Create new user account

uptime
Show uptime

The Ultimate Linux Operating System and Command Line Mastery Guide

until
Execute commands (until error)

unshar
Unpack shell archive scripts

unset
Remove variable or function names

unrar
Extract files from a rar archive

units
Convert units from one scale to another

uniq
Uniquify files

unexpand
Convert spaces to tabs

uname
Print system information

unalias
Remove an alias

umount
Unmount a device

umask
Users file creation mask

ulimit
Limit user resources •

type
Describe a command

tty
Print filename of terminal on stdin

tsort
Topological sort

true
Do nothing, successfully

trap
Run a command when a signal is set(bourne)

traceroute
Trace Route to Host

tr
Translate, squeeze, and/or delete characters

tput
Set terminal-dependent capabilities, color, position

touch
Change file timestamps

top
List processes running on the system

times
User and system times

timeout
Run a command with a time limit

time
Measure Program running time

test
Evaluate a conditional expression

tee
Redirect output to multiple files

tar
Store, list or extract files in an archive

The Ultimate Linux Operating System and Command Line Mastery Guide

tail
Output the last part of file

sync
Synchronize data on disk with memory

suspend
Suspend execution of this shell

sum
Print a checksum for a file

sudo
Execute a command as another user

su
Substitute user identity

strace
Trace system calls and signals

stat
Display file or file system status

ssh
Secure Shell client

split
Split a file into fixed-size pieces

source
Run commands from a file

sort
Sort text files

slocate
Find files

sleep
Delay for a specified time

shutdown
Shutdown or restart linux

shopt
Shell Options

shift
Shift positional parameters

sftp
Secure File Transfer Program

set
Manipulate shell variables and functions

seq
Print numeric sequences

select
Accept keyboard input

sed
Stream Editor

sdiff
Merge two files interactively

screen
Multiplex terminal, runs remote shells through ssh

scp
Secure copy or create remote file copy

rsync
Remote file copy

rmdir
Remove folder/s

rm
Remove files

The Ultimate Linux Operating System and Command Line Mastery Guide

rev
Reverse lines of a file

return
Exit a shell function

renice
Alter priority of running processes

rename
Rename files

remsync
Synchronize remote files via email

reboot
Reboot the system

readonly
Mark variables/functions as read only

readarray
Read from stdin into an array variable

read
Read a line from standard input

rcp
Copy files between two machines

rar
Archive files with compression

ram
ram disk device

quotacheck
Scan a file system for disk usage

quota
Display disk usage and limits

pwd
Print Working Directory

pv
Monitor the progress of data through a pipe

pushd
Save and then change the current directory

ps
Process status

printf
Format and print data

printenv
Print environment variables

printcap
Printer capability database

pr
Prepare files for printing

popd
Restore the previous value of the current directory

pkill
Kill processes by a full or partial name.

ping
Test a network connection

pathchk
Check file name portability

paste
Merge lines of files

passwd
Modify a user password

The Ultimate Linux Operating System and Command Line Mastery Guide

open
Open a file in its default application

op
Operator access

nslookup
Query Internet name servers interactively

notify-send
Send desktop notifications

nohup
Run a command immune to hangups

nl
Number lines and write files

nice
Set the priority of a command or job

netstat
Networking information

nc
Netcat, read and write data across networks

mv
Move or rename files or directories

mtr
Network diagnostics

mtools
Manipulate MS-DOS files

mount
Mount a file system

most
Browse or page through a text file

more
Display output one screen at a time

mmv
Mass Move and rename file/s

mknod
Make block or character special files

mkisofs
Create an hybrid ISO9660/JOLIET/HFS filesystem

mkfifo
Make FIFOs

mkdir
Create new folder/s

man
Help manual

make
Recompile a group of programs

lsof
List open files

ls
List information about file/s

lprm
Remove jobs from the print queue

lprintq
List the print queue

lprintd
Abort a print job

lprint
Print a file

The Ultimate Linux Operating System and Command Line Mastery Guide

lpr
Off line print

lpc
Line printer control program

look
Display lines beginning with a given string

logout
Exit a login shell

logname
Print current login name

locate
Find files

local
Create variables

ln
Create a symbolic link to a file

link
Create a link to a file

let
Perform arithmetic on shell variables

less
Display output one screen at a time

killall
Kill processes by name

kill
Kill a process by specifying its PID

join
Join lines on a common field

jobs
List active jobs

ip
Routing, devices and tunnels

install
Copy files and set attributes

import
Capture an X server screen and save the image to file

ifup
Start a network interface up

ifdown
Stop a network interface

ifconfig
Configure a network interface

if
Conditionally perform command

id
Print user and group id's

iconv
Convert the character set of a file

htop
Interactive process viewer

hostname
Print or set system name

history
Command History

help
Display help for a built-in command

The Ultimate Linux Operating System and Command Line Mastery Guide

head
Output the first part of file/s

hash
Remember the full pathname of a name argument

gzip
Deompress or compress named file/s

groups
Print group names a user is in

groupmod
Modify a group

groupdel
Delete a group

groupadd
Add a user security group

grep
Search file/s for lines matching a given pattern

getopts
Parse positional parameters

gawk
Find and Replace text within file/s

fuser
Identify/kill the process that is accessing a file

function
Define Function Macros

ftp
File Transfer Protocol

fsck
File system consistency check and repair

free
Display memory usage

format
Format disks or tapes

for
Expand words, and execute commands

fold
Wrap text to fit a specified width.

fmt
Reformat paragraph text

find
Search for files that meet a desired criteria

file
Determine file type

fgrep
Search file/s for lines that match a fixed string

fg
Send job to foreground

fdisk
Partition table manipulator for Linux

fdformat
Low-level format a floppy disk

false
Do nothing, unsuccessfully

expr
Evaluate expressions

export
Set an environment variable

The Ultimate Linux Operating System and Command Line Mastery Guide

expect
Automate arbitrary applications that are accessed over a terminal

expand
Convert tabs into spaces

exit
Exit the shell

exec
Execute a command

eval
Evaluate several commands/arguments

ethtool
Ethernet card settings

env
Environment variables

enable
Enable and disable builtin shell commands

eject
Eject removable media

egrep
Search file(s) for lines that match an extended expression

echo
Display message on screen

du
Estimate file space usage

dmesg
Print kernel & driver messages

dirs
Display list of remembered directories

dirname
Convert a full pathname to just a path

dircolors
Colour setup for `ls'

dir
Briefly list directory contents

dig
DNS lookup

diff3
Show differences among three files

diff
Display the differences between two files

df
Display free disk space

declare
Declare variables and give them attributes

ddrescue
Data recovery tool

dd
Convert and copy a file, write disk headers, boot records

dc
Desk Calculator

date
Display or change the date & time

cut
Divide a file into several parts

curl
Transfer data from or to a server

The Ultimate Linux Operating System and Command Line Mastery Guide

csplit
Split a file into context-determined pieces

crontab
Schedule a command to run at a later time

cron
Daemon to execute scheduled commands

cp
Copy one or more files to another location

continue
Resume the next iteration of a loop

command
Run a command - ignoring shell functions

comm
Compare two sorted files line by line

cmp
Compare two files

clear
Clear terminal screen

cksum
Print CRC checksum and byte counts

chroot
Run a command with a different root directory

chown
Change file owner and group

chmod
Change access permissions

chkconfig
System services

chgrp
Change group ownership

cfdisk
Partition table manipulator for Linux

cd
Change Directory

cat
Concatenate and print the content of files

case
Conditionally perform command

cal
Display a calendar

bzip2
Decompress or compress named file/s

builtin
Run a shell builtin

break
Exit from a loop •

bind
Set or display readline key and function bindings •

bg
Send to background

bc
Arbitrary precision calculator language

bash
GNU Bourne-Again SHell

basename
Strip directory and suffix from filenames

The Ultimate Linux Operating System and Command Line Mastery Guide

awk
Find and Replace text, database sort/validate/index

aspell
spell Checker

aptitude
Search for and install software packages (Debian/Ubuntu)

apt-get
Search for and install software packages (Debian/Ubuntu)

apropos
search help manual pages

alias
Create an alias

.
Run a command script in the current shell

###

Comment / Remark

!!

Run the last command again

Numbers
Of course, you can expect that numbers are used to store numerical values.
Assign your preferred numbers to the variables. For example:

var1 = 1
var2 = 10

You can also make use of the following numerical types:
1. Int (signed integers)
2. Complex (complex numbers)
3. Float (floating real point values)
4. Long (long integers; could be hexadecimal and octal)

Lists

Linux also allows you to create lists that could be enclosed in brackets {[]}. They are like the same lists used in C Language, but are definitely easier to make. Again, make use of slice operators ([] or [:]), and start with indexes of 0. You can concentrate the strings by using the plus sign (+) and repeat by using the asterisk (*).

Dictionaries

In Linux, Dictionaries are considered as hash tables or associative arrays. They are filled up with numbers and strings. They are enclosed by curly braces {{}} and values are assigned by square braces [].

Linux Classes

Classes determine the scope of the program, which are:
Local names, or innermost scope;
Built-in names and words last searched, or outermost scope;
Current global module names or next to last scope, and;
Enclosing Function scope.

Loops

There are three types of loops and they are:

For Loop. This is when statements are executed a multiple number of times and codes are abbreviated.

While Loop. This is when statements or groups of statements are repeated when conditions are said to be true.

Nested Loop. This means you're using loops inside or above the first few loops.

You can also make use of Loop Control Statements, such as:

Continue Statement. This makes the loop skip the rest of its body and resets it back to its original form.

Break Statement. This transfers statement execution before terminating the loop, and immediately brings back the other loop. For example:

Pass Statement. When you do not want to execute codes or commands for syntax, that's what you call a pass statement.

Tuple

A Tuple is like list data but is composed of a lot of values that are separated by commas, and are enclosed in parentheses () as opposed to brackets. Tuples also cannot be updated.

Data Type Conversion

Unichr (x). And finally, with this command, you'll get a Unicode character.
Tuple (t). Converts x to tuple.
Str (x). converts x to string representation.
Set (s). Converts x to set.
Repr (x). Converts x to repression string.
Ord (x). This gives a single character its integer value.
Oct (x). Converts x to octal string.
Long (x [,base]). Converts x to long integers.
List (L). Converts x to list.
Int (x [,base]). If x is a string, it becomes the base; also converts x to an integer.
Hex (x). Converts x to hexadecimal string.
Frozen set (s). Converts x to frozen set.
Float (x). Converts integers into floating numbers.
Eval (str). This evaluates a string and gives you an object in return.
Dict (d). This gives you a dictionary.
Complex (real [,imag]). This gives you a complex number.

Assigning the Right Values

The equal sign (=) is important here because. You do not need to make explicit declarations here but you have to make sure that you place the variable before the equal sign, and on the right, put what you want to happen to the variable.

Statements and Loops
There are three types of loops and they are:

For Loop. This is when statements are executed a multiple number of times and codes are abbreviated.

While Loop. This is when statements or groups of statements are repeated when conditions are said to be true.

Nested Loop. This means you're using loops inside or above the first few loops.

You can also make use of Loop Control Statements, such as:

Continue Statement. This makes the loop skip the rest of its body and resets it back to its original form.

Break Statement. This transfers statement execution before terminating the loop, and immediately brings back the other loop. For example:

Pass Statement. When you do not want to execute codes or commands for syntax, that's what you call a pass statement.

Comparison Operators
==. Condition equates to true if the operands are equal. ((a==b) is not true)
<>. If values are not equal, condition becomes true. ((a<>b) is true)
!=. Condition becomes true if values of two operands are not equal.
<=. Condition becomes true if left operand value is less than the right operand. (a <=b) is true)
>=. Condition becomes true if value of left operand is greater than right operand. (a>=b) is not true)
<. If left operand value is less than right operand, condition is true. (a < b) is true)
>. If value of left operand is greater than right, condition is true. ((a>b is not true)

Special Codes and Characters
In order to program those, you have to make use of special characters and codes. These are:

Built-in String Method

Zfill (width). Left-pads original string with zeros.
Upper (). Turns lowercase letters into uppercase.
Translate (table, deletechars="") Turns string into translation table.
Title (). Turns string into titlecard version, which means uppercase becomes lowercase and vice-versa.
Swapcase (). All letters in the string will be inverted.
Strip ([chars]). Performs rstrip() and Istrip() on each string.
Startswith (str, beg=0, end=len (string)). Checks whether string is string itself or subset of string.

The Ultimate Linux Operating System and Command Line Mastery Guide

Splitlines (num=string.count('\n')). Returns each of the line with new strings.

Split (str="", num=string.count (str)). Splits the strings into delimeters.

Rjust (width, [,fillchar]). This gives you space-padded strings.

Rindex (str, beg=0, end=len(string)). This is just like index but with backward string.

Replace (old, new [max]). This replaces current string with max occurrences.

Max (str). This returns max character alphabetical string.

Join (seq). This merges representations of the strings.

Isdecimal(). If Unicode string contains decimal characters, value returns as true; false otherwise.

Find (str, beg=0, end=len(string)). This checks whether str is on string or on subsequent string.

Expandtabs (tabsize = 8). Strings and tabs are then placed in multiple spaces.

Encode (suffix, beg=0, end=len(string)). This runs an encoded version of each string.

Decode (encoding UTF-8, errors=strict). The codec registered for encoding will be used for this method, and you'd get a default string.

Count (str, beg=0, end=len(string)). This counts the number of times a string appears and begins indexing.

Center (width, fillchar). Along with the original string, this'll give you a space-padded string consuming the total width of the columns.

Capitalize(). This basically capitalizes the first letter of the string.

Format Symbols and their Functions

%X hexadecimal integer (UPPERcase letters)
%x hexadecimal integer (lowercase letters)
%u unsigned decimal integer
%s string conversion via str() prior to formatting
%o octal integer
%i signed decimal integer
%g the shorter of %f and %e
%G the shorter of %f and %E
%f floating point real number
%E exponential notation (with UPPERcase 'E')
%e exponential notation (with lowercase 'e')
%d signed decimal integer
%c character

Other Important Symbols

m.n.m is the minimum total width and n is the number of digits to display after the decimal point (if appl.)

0. pad from left with zeros (instead of spaces)

<sp>. leave a blank space before a positive number

+. display the sign

*. argument specifies width or precision

(var). mapping variable (dictionary arguments)

%. '%%' leaves you with a single literal '%'

#. add octal leading zero ('0') or the hexadecimal leading '0x' or '0X', depending on whether 'x' or 'X' were used.

-. left justification

The Ultimate Linux Operating System and Command Line Mastery Guide

CHAPTER 8 MANAGING FILES AND DIRECTORIES

Managing Linux files and directories would help you keep things in check. As with any kind of OS, it is important to make sure that you know what's happening to your system so that it would not disintegrate. More so, it is a way of being mindful of the things you have in your system. Learn more about them in this chapter.

Directories of Addresses

As the name suggests, this is a telecommunications protocol that makes it easy for communication apps and websites to work. It is used to map network addresses, making messaging—and even video calls—possible, and has also been used for important technologies, such as Xerox PARC Universal Packet, DEC Net, ChaosNet, and IPv4, among others. For this, you can keep in mind the following:

1. 0 – Hardware Type (HTYPE)
2. 2 – Protocol Type (PTYPE)
3. 4 – Hardware Address (HLEN) | Protocol Address (PLEN)
4. 6 – Operation (OPER)
5. 8 – Sender Hardware Address (SHA)
6. 10 - Next 2 succeeding bytes
7. 12 – Last 2 succeeding bytes
8. 14 – Sender Address Protocol (SAP)
9. 16 – last 2 succeeding bytes
10. 18 – Target Hardware Address (THA)
11. 20 – next 2 succeeding bytes
12. 22 – last 2 succeeding bytes
13. 24 – Target Protocol Address (TPA)
14. 26 – last 2 succeeding bytes

Transport Directories

The Transport Directories contain the channels of data that are involved in Linux, which also establish process-to-process connectivity and end-to-end message transfers that provide the right information and logistics for any specific purpose in the network. This could either be implemented, connectionless, or object-oriented.

The port is then established with the help of the transport layer where logical constructs are around. It basically means that:

1. Data should be correct—and could only have minimal error;
2. Data should arrive in order;
3. Data should include traffic congestion control;
4. Packets that are discarded or lost have to be resent, and;
5. Duplicate data has to be discarded.

When that happens, you can expect even the newest version of the Stream Control Protocol to work properly in your network. You don't have to rely on connectionless datagrams, though, because as the name suggests, they don't offer the right connections—and are quite unreliable.

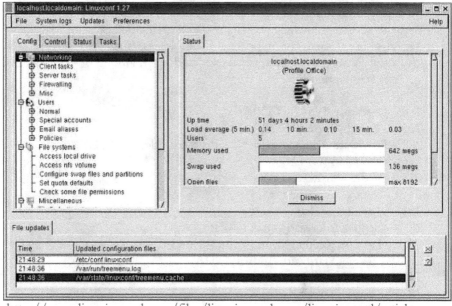

http://www.linuxjournal.com/files/linuxjournal.com/linuxjournal/articles /059/5918/5918f1.jpg

Application Directories

The Application Directories encapsulates the protocols used by services that provide exchanging applications. This also includes host configuration protocols, routing services and network support services. Examples include File Transfer Protocol (FTP), Hypertext Transfer Protocol (HTTP), and Dynamic Host Configuration Protocol (DHCP). This way, you would be able to lower data transfer based on the protocols you are using.

Application layer also treats the Transport Directories as a stable network with black boxes that allow communication to happen all throughout the application, while making sure that key qualities of each part of the application still works as strong as it can. Whatever happens to the Application Directories does not concern the Transport and Internet layers because traffic does not usually examine the said layer. However, sometimes, it is essential for the NAT, or Network Address Translator, to consider the payload of the application—and make sure that things are running smoothly.

Link Directories

The networking methods are defined within the link layer. The scope is the intervening routers, together with the host network, including the protocols that are being used to describe the topology of the network, and datagrams are also evident with various goals and assumptions together with strict layering. This means that you can implement Linux above any hardware network technology.

With the help of the link layer, packets could easily be moved and could receive driver card packets, and it also means that the layer corresponds to the OSI model.

Internet Directories

Basically, the Internet Directories works in such a way that it holds responsibility over sending the right packets, and making sure that they could move across several networks. Its main functions are:

1. **Packet Routing.** This is all about sending packets of data from the destination's source, all the way to where it needs to be used. Unique Protocol Numbers identify these.

2. **Host Identification and Addressing.** With the help of a hierarchical IP System, this one is achieved.

Directory 5 to 10

These are used to resolve the host because they work under the syntax LinuxConnector::resolvehostname() and they are able to convert IP Addresses and host names with the help of getaddridinfo() function. This is way better than just gethostname() because it is known as a safe thread.

Directory 13 to 15

These lines are collectively known as LinuxConnector::resolvehost. They're able to convert the name string and DNS Host to an IP Address so that every assumption made could be converted to different network addresses.

Directory 16

This is the socket() first argument so that you could select specifics and choose protocol families of the communication networks. SOCK_STREAM and PF_INET should be used as they work well together.

Directory 17 to 20

These are known as connect::passing() because it points the user to the right structure with the help of sockaddr_in pointers. It will help you know how long the structure is so that you would not confuse it with the other functions of the program and the network itself.

Lines 28 to 34

These make use of the listen() function. Basically, you could make TCP Requests and have them queued for you to support participating branches of your network. Some Operating Systems do not support this, though, but then you could just try using the function m_listening.

Lines 23 to 27

These are able to bind the listening socket by returning the proper message/bind() values.

Lines 20 to 21

These allow you to listen to the IP and search for connections even abruptly after certain connections end. However, you can disable this by making use of SO_REUSEADDR function.

Lines 21 to 32

This gives you in indefinite and continuous number of connections from the clients, and also helps you process a good number of bytes from them, too. It uses the syntax LinuxAcceptor::start where you could also process a number of bites from the client. Zero (0) appears when there are no available clients—and servers—around.

Lines 12 to 20

These gives you command-line arguments with the TCPAcceptor function. Take note that you do have to specify the IP Address for the server to start making connections.

Lines 5 to 10

These lines will help you realize that the server would start listening to the IP Port and that there would be a command line between the important IP Addresses. Error Messages would be displayed when the user tries to invoke the wrong information.

Lines 13 to 18

With these, you'll know whether the server is listening or not because it uses m_address. It also puts and converts bytes into order and prevents socket failures while listening is in order.

Lines 9 to 12

These will help you initialize new sockets in your network by making use of the PF_INET protocol. TCP Port will come in order, too.

Line 7

This will help you create the description for the socket so that you could create different calls for different sockets.

Lines 3 to 10

Meanwhile, if you are trying to accept connections from your clients, these lines will come in handy. For these, the TCPAcceptor::accept syntax is extremely useful. This way, you get all the qualified functions in one thread and you won't get confused.

Encapsulation Directory

Now, in order to provide Linux with its much-needed abstraction layers,

Encapsulation is done. It is aligned with the protocol suite's functional division so that each level would be properly encapsulated and dealt with.

Take note that whatever is on top of the layer are those that are closely used in the user applications themselves. However, there is no single architectural model that has to be followed, especially when you have less-defined models such as the OSI model. This is its main difference from other internet protocols, especially the earlier ones.

The Ultimate Linux Operating System and Command Line Mastery Guide

CHAPTER 9 ADMINISTRATION AND SECURITY

To help you gain better security, and make sure your OS would always be in a "healthy" state, it's best that you take note of the commands given below:

Protocol of User Datagrams

This is an important member of the Internet Protocol Suite. It provides connectionless transmissions in such a way that they could actually be reliable, and that they would not ruin the protocol of the network in any way. They are perfect for time-sensitive applications that easily drop pockets. User Diagram Protocols are also:

1. It is capable of providing datagrams to the network;

2. It is transaction-oriented and work for both Network Time Protocols and Domain Name Systems;

3. It works with unidirectional communication, which is suitable for service discoveries and broadcast information;

4. It works for real-time applications (such as Twitter, Snapchat, Periscope, etc.) because it makes way of transmission delays. It also works for VOIP applications (such as Skype), and works for some games, as well;

5. It is suitable for a large number of clients, and is stateless. It also works for streaming applications, and;

6. It's perfect for bootstrapping because it is simple and stateless.
It also works for Octets 0 to 4, and even 20 to 160 in some cases.

Cross Platforms

You could also do cross-platform programming for Linux. For this, you have to keep the following in mind:

1. windows.h and winsock.h should be used as the header files.

2. Instead of close(), closesocket() has to be used.

3. Send () and Receive() are used, instead of read() or write().

4. WSAStartup() is used to initialize the library.

Protocols of Aliases

Another important protocol of Linux, this one could send requested services and messages to the router, and also has its own protocol number. The difference is that it starts in the IPv4 Header, and is mostly just known as '1'. It also works between octets 0 to 4, where:

1. Code = Control Messages | ICMP Subtype

2. Type = Control Messages | ICMP Subtype

3. Rest of Header = Contents | ICMP Subtype

4. Checksum = Error Checking Data | ICMP Header and Data

Data then derives a section in IPv4 where error-checking is done. Implementations are also accessible through APIs and various kinds of sockets, together with Network Discovery Protocols and microcontroller firmware.

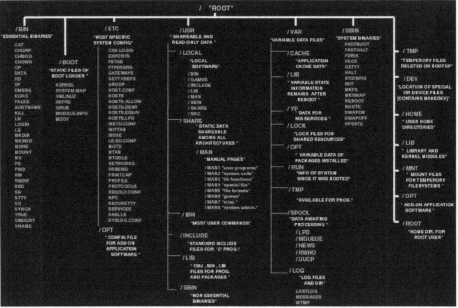

https://www.blackmoreops.com/wp-content/uploads/2015/02/Linux-file-system-hierarchy-Linux-file-structure-blackMORE-Ops.jpg

The Ultimate Linux Operating System and Command Line Mastery Guide

Internet Message Protocol

What you have to understand about Linux is that it is an Open System Interconnect (OSI) Internet Model which means that it works in sockets (). In order to establish connections, you need to make use of listening sockets so that the host could make calls—or in other words, connections.

By inputting listen (), the user will be able to accept () blocks on the program. This binds () the program together and makes it whole. Now, to make things clearer, you have to understand the basic model of the internet.

The Internet Model combines session, presentation, and application of layers and the ports of the TCP, making way of bind() to happen. Now, you also have to wait from the response from both the sender and the receiver. This makes it easy for the exchange of requests and messages to be done until the connection is closed. When done properly, the sender and receiver won't have to worry about messages getting unsent, or communications getting cut.

Connections could then be contained in just one thread so that it would not be too complicated for the network to understand. This way, the right Protocol Stacks could be created, too.

Working on Transmissions

This provides error-checked, orderly, and reliable stream of octets between the IP Network and the various networks that it contains. This is used for email, and most of the World Wide Web, as well. This is also a latent, connectionless protocol, and works by processing data that has already been transmitted. It works from octets 0 to 160, containing source and destination ports. It also contains sequence numbers, and acknowledgment numbers.

Data Offset is also reserved, together with window size, checksum, and urgent pointers, as well.

Basically, what you can keep in mind is:

1. 16 bits identify the source port;

2. 16 bits also identify the receiving port;

3. 4 bits specify the data header in 32-bit words;

4. 32 bits identify the acknowledgment numbers;

5. 9-bits contain the 9-bit flags;

6. 3 bits define data that is reserved for future use.

Other bits define options that you could create for your app or website using this OS.

Host Resolutions

One thing you have to keep in mind about this is that you should use the syntax gethostname() so the standard library could make the right call. This also happens when you're trying to look for the name of a certain part of the program, and when you want to use it for larger applications. It's almost the same as python as you could code it this way

Linux Sockets

What you have to understand about Linux is that it is an Open System Interconnect (OSI) Internet Model which means that it works in sockets (). In order to establish connections, you need to make use of listening sockets so that the host could make calls—or in other words, connections.

By inputting listen (), the user will be able to accept () blocks on the program. This binds () the program together and makes it whole. For this, you could keep the following in mind:

Server: socket() □ bind() □ listen() □ accept() □ read() □ write() □ read()
Send Request: write() □ read()
Receive Reply: write() □ read()
Establish connections: connect □ accept()
Close Connection: close() □ read()
Client: socket() □ connect □ write() □ read() □ close()

Linux Internet Protocols

Internet Protocol is all about providing boundaries in the network, as well as relaying datagrams that allow internet-networking to happen.

The construction involves a header and a payload where the header is known to be the main IP Address, and with interfaces that are connected with the help of certain parameters. Routing prefixes and network designation are also involved, together with internal or external gateway protocols, too. Reliability also depends on end-to-end protocols, but mostly, you could expect the framework to be this way:

UDP Header | UDP DATA □ Transport
IP Header | IP Data □ Internet
Frame Header | Frame Data | Frame Footer □ Link
Data □ Application

Getting Peer Information

In order to get peer information, you have to make sure that you return both TCP and IP information. This way, you could be sure that both server and client are connected to the network. You could also use the getpeername() socket so that when information is available, it could easily be captured and saved. This provides the right data to be sent and received by various methods involved in Linux, and also contains proper socket descriptors and grants privileges to others in the program. Some may even be deemed private, to make the experience better for the users.

To accept information, let the socket TCPAcceptor::accept() be prevalent in the network. This way, you could differentiate actions coming from the server and the client.

Construct and Destruct

These are connected to the descriptor of the socket that allow peer TCP Ports and peer IP Addresses to show up onscreen. Take note that this does not use other languages, except for C++, unlike its contemporaries in Linux.
Destructors are then able to close any connections that you have made. For example, if you want to log out of one of your social networking accounts, you're able to do it because destructors are around.

Linux and SMTP Clients

As for SMTP Client, you could expect that it involves some of the same characters above—with just a few adjustments. You also should keep in mind that this is all about opening the socket, opening input and output streams, reading and writing the socket, and lastly, cleaning the client portal up. You also have to know that it involves the following:

1. **Datagram Communication.** This means that local sockets would work every time your portal sends datagrams to various clients and servers.

2. **Linux Communications.** This time, stream and datagram communication are involved.

3. **Programming Sockets.** And of course, you can expect you'll program sockets in the right manner!

Echo Client Set-ups

In Linux, Echo Clients work by means of inserting arguments inside the socket() because it means that you will be able to use the IP together with the PF_INET function so that they could both go in the TCP socket. To set up a proper client structure, just remember you have to make a couple of adjustments from earlier codes.

IO Network Models

In order to get peer information, you have to make sure that you return both TCP and IP information. This way, you could be sure that both server and client are connected to the network. You could also use the getpeername() socket so that when information is available, it could easily be captured and saved.

To accept information, let the socket LinuxAcceptor::accept() be prevalent in the network. This way, you could differentiate actions coming from the server and the client.

Linux and its Sockets

You also have to understand that you can code Linux in C mainly because they both involve the use of sockets. the socket works like a bridge that binds the client to the port, and is also responsible for sending the right kinds of requests to the server while waiting for it to respond. Finally, sending and receiving of data is done.

At the same time, the Linux Socket is also able to create a socket for the server that would then bind itself to the port. During that stage, you can begin listening to client traffic as it builds up. You could also wait for the client at that point, and finally, see the sending and receiving of data to

The Ultimate Linux Operating System and Command Line Mastery Guide

happen. Its other functions are the following:

socket_description. This allows the description of both the client and the server will show up onscreen.

write buffer. This describes the data that needs to be sent.

write buffer length. In order to write the buffer length, you'll have to see the string's output.

client_socket. The socket description will also show on top.
address. This is used for the connect function so that address_len would be on top.

address_len. If the second parameter is null, this would appear onscreen.

return. This helps return description of both the client and the socket. This also lets interaction become easy between the client and the server.

server_socket. This is the description of the socket that's located on top.

backlog. This is the amount of requests that have not yet been dealt with. You could also put personal comments every once in a while—but definitely not all the time!

CONCLUSION

Thank you for reading this book!

Hopefully, with the help of this book, you have learned what you need to learn about Linux—and what it entails.

Do try the tips mentioned in this book, and let this book serve as your guide when it comes to using and understanding Linux.

Finally, if you enjoyed this book, kindly post a short review on Amazon. It will be greatly appreciated.

Thank you, and enjoy!

The Ultimate Linux Operating System and Command Line Mastery Guide

Check Out My Other Books

Congratulations on learning a new operating system. Now the next step would be to continue to practice your new skills and I would like to strongly recommend that you learn other software and programming languages.

OTHER BOOKS
WINDOWS 10 MASTERY – THE ULTIMATE WINDOWS 10 MASTERY GUIDE

I have also have more books that are part of my "A Code Like a Pro" series that you can download.

--Here are the Links to my other books:. –

A CODE LIKE A PRO BOOK SERIES
PYTHON MASTERY – A CODE LIKE A PRO GUIDE FOR PYTHON BEGINNERS

ANGULARJS – A CODE LIKE A PRO GUIDE

HACKING MASTERY – A CODE LIKE A PRO GUIDE FOR COMPUTER HACKING BEGINNERS

If the links do not work, for whatever reason, you can simply search for these titles on the Amazon website to find them.